LET'S CLEAN UP!

By JENNA LAFFIN

Illustrated by TINA KUGLER

CANTATA
LEARNING

MANKATO, MINNESOTA

WWW.CANTATALEARNING.COM

CANTATA LEARNING

MANKATO, MINNESOTA

Published by Cantata Learning
1710 Roe Crest Drive
North Mankato, MN 56003
www.cantatalearning.com

Library of Congress Control Number: 2014956992
978-1-63290-256-6 (hardcover/CD)
978-1-63290-408-9 (paperback/CD)
978-1-63290-450-8 (paperback)

Let's Clean Up! by Jenna Laffin
Illustrated by Tina Kugler

Book design, Tim Palin Creative
Editorial direction, Flat Sole Studio
Executive musical production and direction, Elizabeth Draper
Music arranged and produced by Musical Youth Productions

Printed in the United States of America.

VISIT

WWW.CANTATALEARNING.COM/ACCESS-OUR-MUSIC

TO SING ALONG TO THE SONG

Keeping spaces you use **tidy** and clean is important. **Clutter** makes it hard to find things and move around. Spills and messes can stink. They can also hold **germs** that can make people sick.

Now turn the page, and sing along.

I clean up.

You clean up.

Let's clean up!

Clean the table
and clean the chair.

8

Wash the dishes
and clear the stairs.

If it's icky,
clean it up.

10

If it's sticky,
clean it up.

I clean up.

You clean up.

Let's clean up!

Put things away
so people don't trip.

14

And wipe up spills
so we don't slip!

15

16

If it's smelly,
clean it up.

If it's messy,
clean it up.

Clean your room
and clean at school.

Use your hands
and cleaning tools.

I clean up.

You clean up.

Let's clean up!

BACK TO SCHOOL BARBEQUE

GUIDED READING ACTIVITIES

1. In three sentences or less, write a summary of this story.

2. What types of things do you have to clean up at home?

3. Set a timer to three minutes or play a song. Then see how much you can clean up before the timer stops or the song is done.

Clean His Room. Mankato, MN: Picture Window Books, 2013. Print.

e Park. Mankato, MN: Picture Window Books, 2012. Print.

w to Clean Your Room in 10 Easy Steps. New York: Schwartz & Wade Books, 2010. Print.

Up. Mankato, MN: Child's World, 2009. Print.

SONG LYRICS
Let's Clean Up!

I clean up.
You clean up.
Let's clean up!

Clean the table,
and clean the chair.
Wash the dishes
and clear the stairs.

If it's icky,
clean it up.
If it's sticky,
clean it up.

I clean up.
You clean up.
Let's clean up!

Put things away,
so people don't trip.
And wipe up spills,
so we don't slip!

If it's smelly,
clean it up.
If it's messy,
clean it up.

Clean your room,
and clean at school.
Use your hands
and cleaning tools.

I clean up.
You clean up.
Let's clean up!

Let's Clean Up!

Chorus

I clean up.
You clean up.
Let's

Clean the ta-ble, and clean the chair. Wash the dish-es

If it's ick-y, clean it up. If it's stick-y,

Chorus

Verse 2
Put things away, so people don't trip.
And wipe up spills, so we don't slip!

If it's smelly, clean it up.
If it's messy, clean it up.

Verse 3 (short
Clean your ro
Use your han

Chorus

SONG LYRICS
Let's Clean Up!

I clean up.
You clean up.
Let's clean up!

Clean the table,
and clean the chair.
Wash the dishes
and clear the stairs.

If it's icky,
clean it up.
If it's sticky,
clean it up.

I clean up.
You clean up.
Let's clean up!

Put things away,
so people don't trip.
And wipe up spills,
so we don't slip!

If it's smelly,
clean it up.
If it's messy,
clean it up.

Clean your room,
and clean at school.
Use your hands
and cleaning tools.

I clean up.
You clean up.
Let's clean up!

Pop/Zydeco
Musical Youth Productions

Let's Clean Up!

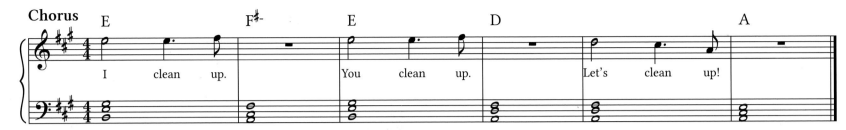

Chorus

Verse 2
Put things away, so people don't trip.
And wipe up spills, so we don't slip!

If it's smelly, clean it up.
If it's messy, clean it up.

Verse 3 (short verse)
Clean your room, and clean at school.
Use your hands and cleaning tools.

Chorus

GLOSSARY

clutter—a large amount of things that are not sitting in a neat way

germs—tiny living things that can cause illness

tidy—clean and neat

GUIDED READING ACTIVITIES

1. In three sentences or less, write a summary of this story.

2. What types of things do you have to clean up at home?

3. Set a timer to three minutes or play a song. Then see how much you can clean up before the timer stops or the song is done.

TO LEARN MORE

Bracken, Beth. *Henry Helps Clean His Room*. Mankato, MN: Picture Window Books, 2013. Print.

Ghigna, Charles. *Pick Up the Park*. Mankato, MN: Picture Window Books, 2012. Print.

Huget, Jennifer LaRue. *How to Clean Your Room in 10 Easy Steps*. New York: Schwartz & Wade Books, 2010. Print.

Minden, Cecilia. *Cleaning Up*. Mankato, MN: Child's World, 2009. Print.